ALIYAH RYDELL
BEYOND ORDER

The Ultimate Guide on Best Organization Tips, Discover Simple and Easy to Learn Strategies on How to Get and Keep Your Home Organized

Descrierea CIP a Bibliotecii Naționale a României
ALIYAH RYDELL
    BEYOND ORDER. The Ultimate Guide on Best Organization Tips, Discover Simple and Easy to Learn Strategies on How to Get and Keep Your Home Organized / Aliyah Rydell – Bucharest: Editura My Ebook, 2021
    ISBN

ALIYAH RYDELL

BEYOND ORDER

The Ultimate Guide on Best Organization Tips, Discover Simple and Easy to Learn Strategies on How to Get and Keep Your Home Organized

My Ebook Publishing House
Bucharest, 2021

TABLE OF CONTENTS

Introduction	7
Remembering to Organize	11
Say Good-bye to Clutter	14
Best Secrets to Getting and Staying Organized	16
The Emotional Toll of CLUTTER	20
Turn Clutter into Harmony	25
An Orderly Life	29
Let Good Order Reign!	33
Getting Rid of "Stuff"	37
The Art of Organization	40
A Few Good Organizing Tips and Tricks	43
Determining your Home-Style	46
Clever Home and Family Management	51
Have Time on your Side	54
Organize a Bit at a Time	58
Organize your junk drawer	58

Organize your laundry room	59
Organize your children	60
Organize your garage	64
Organize your child's study habits	67
Organize your kitchen	71
Put the Word "Organize" Back into your Life	74
Timesaving Tips	75
12 Simple Ways to Organize	78
C.O.P.E.	82
Organize your Move	85
Organize your Home Office	87
Organize your Workspace	94
Hire an Organizer	97
Take Control of Chronic Disorganization	100
Smart Time Management Just for Moms	104
A Final Home Organizing	111
The Benefits of Being Organized	115

INTRODUCTION

"You can find pictures anywhere. It is simply a matter of noticing things and organizing them. You just have to care about what is around you and have a concern with humanity and the human comedy."

Elliott Erwitt

How we spend out time says a lot about who we are

If you are simply too tired or do not have adequate time to do anything in the evenings, then your daily routine is out of balance and you need to make adjustments.

Your work can be too difficult or unsuitable, or you may not be making full use of your hours during your day or evening. A good balance of your time is needed for work, goals, recreation, and relaxation. Take a close look at your daily routine, examine your findings and come up with a plan. Be prepared to follow your plan and with this, you can become **better organized.**

Why be better organized?

Being busy will keep your mind off worry because you will not be thinking of two different things at one time. You can make good use of your time away from work to increase your knowledge of things and life, to work at a hobby or project, and then to relax and be content. This is good balance and when you are better balanced your are better organized.

Perhaps you are a single parent and in a bit of a time crunch each day. Make a point to sit and relax each day and plan. If you are careful you should be able to find just a few hours each day to apply yourself to being better organized.

"I know of no more encouraging fact than the unquestionable ability of man to elevate his life by conscious endeavor." - Henry Thoreau (1817-1862)

Most of us use only a small amount of our true capabilities and we can all do so much more. You can learn new things. This will give you new purpose in life and a feeling of achievement. Read nonfiction books to increase your knowledge of everyday things in life and to learn new skills or to improve on existing ones. All of this will help you to be better organized.

The more organized you are the more time you will have for yourself. As you become better organized, take on a new after hours project. Start with something small and work your way up to devoting more and more time to your project. Perhaps you can take on a new woodworking project, for example. Once you complete it, you will feel good about yourself and how you are spending your new, organized time.

With a place for everything and everything in its place, you are freed up in body and mind to take on new endeavors.

If you are under a lot of stress, a more passive and relaxing undertaking might be just what you need, at least to start with. For just one day a week, or a few hours on certain days, set aside time for your own unique enjoyment. When you do this, staying organized will not feel as much of a chore. You will naturally wish to remain organized so that you will have more time for yourself.

Take a walk in the park, listen to lovely music, read an interesting novel, leisurely work in the yard, or watch a bit of TV, these are all of the perks in time from staying organized.

"When I go into my garden with a spade, and dig a bed, I feel such an exhilaration and health that I discover that I have been defrauding myself all this time in letting others do for me what I should have done with my own hands." - Ralph Waldo Emerson (1803-1882)

Remembering to Organize

Being well organized takes lots of time and effort and there is a lot to remember. Below are good tips to help you to remember it all:

1. *Jot it down.* With the many details that you have to remember in any given day, why should you try to keep it all in a memory bank? At the very moment that you remember something needs to be done, the very best thing to do is write it down. Then, just as you need to recall it, it will be there for you in an instant.

2. *Keep it all in one place.* Once you have developed the knack of writing everything down, your next step will be to keep your writing all in one place. You will remember better this way. Otherwise, you are going to spend valuable time searching for your notes.

3. *Stay healthy.* A keen memory is a well-nourished mind. Eat healthy; get plenty of rest and lots of good exercise. These

will all see you through to having a good memory, staying focused and being alert.

4. *Record your every thought.* You might find yourself driving when a good idea about organizing comes to you or you might recall something that you really need to write down. No need to pull over and start writing, record instead! Pull off to the side of the road and use a small hand held tape recorder. This is a wonderful tool to carry around with you, to record your thoughts, or your parking space number, or even a memorable telephone number you see on a billboard as you drive by. Use your handy recorder to be your second eyes and ears.

5. *Call ahead.* When you are at the office and you want to do something when you arrive back home, call ahead to your answering machine and leave yourself a message. As soon as you get home you can listen to your message and remember exactly what you wanted to do.

6. *Be confident in yourself.* If you keep saying you have a bad memory, you will probably continue to have a bad memory. It is important to have a motivated, I CAN remember attitude.

7. *Handy email reminders.* There are many good and free e-mail reminder services available. You can type in what you want to remember, such as a welcome party, anniversary or special event, and you will receive an e-mail reminder when the

date is approaching. This is a terrific way to jog your memory by Internet.

8. *Use sticky notes.* Those wonderful, little sticky notes are the next best thing to sliced bread! They are amazing as memory helpers. Want to remember something prior to leaving your home? Just mark it down on a Post-It Note and stick it to the inside of your door. The bright, neon colors will be great to catch your eye as you are leaving. You will not likely miss it! Need to make an urgent call first thing in the morning? Leave a Post-It Note on your telephone.

9. *Use timers and alarms.* Take advantage of alarm clocks and timers throughout your day. Have to take the clothes out of the dryer by 12 noon? Set your alarm clock to remind you. Want to leave for the ladies luncheon by 7 p.m.? Set your timer to beep a few minutes before it is time to start to get ready.

10. *Visual memory joggers.* Visual reminders will help you remember and stay focused. Use visual reminders for remembering your goals. If your goal is to take a trip to a Ireland in a few years, keep a magazine photograph of Ireland right on your desk. If your goal is to lose 30 lbs. in six months, find a picture or ornament that will help remind you of this goal each day.

Say Good-bye to Clutter

Now that you have a good system to remember your tasks at hand, the next big step will be to get rid of clutter. Clutter diminishes a smile, dampens the spirit, and so should not be tolerated.

It is very easy to find any given room in a cluttered mess, but it takes some hard work to de-clutter and organize.

Many people say that one of their favorite things to do when stressed out is to clean! Hard to imagine, right? Well, it is true. Cleaning gives order and purpose to your life, even if only in smaller chunks at a time.

We are not just talking about moving around clutter from one shelf to another. We are talking about de-cluttering every room of your home. Say good-bye to the dust, say good-bye to the junk – say hello to room to breathe and move around! Now, doesn't that sound delightful?

Start out by drawing up a list of what you absolutely want done. Think about those leaning tower of Pisa papers in the den, then move slowly into the family room. See any piles of old photos just crying out to be placed in a photo album? Write that one down. How about those piles of clothing sitting in the bottom of your daughters closet just waiting for a mother's touch. Write that one down, too!

By now, if you are clever, you see a list of very workable, one-at-a-time chores that can be assigned throughout a busy day. The idea is to get started and work your way around. By the end of the day, you will have a beautiful, uncluttered home as your reward!

Do not become discouraged if your attempt to enlist your husband and children runs a-muck. Just write them down on your list as those who require an attitude adjustment and then save that chore for next time. One can hope!

If you are altogether frank about it, you really do not want a second pair of meddling hands anyway; some chores are best left to only one pair of hands. That way you can be sure that the chores will be done right the first time.

Best Secrets to Getting and Staying Organized

➤ Tell yourself (and believe) that some degree of clutter with a child is going to happen no matter what!

➤ Begin with messes and clutter that you see every day. Work on organizing your kitchen and family room before your hallway closet.

➤ Assign everything in your house a place. This way when your family searches for something they need, they will know exactly where to find it and where to put it away.

➤ Use this same principle to organize your silverware, with clearly defined places for every fork and knife, or drawers for ties and socks or, underwear. Think in this same way for every aspect of your home. This will save many hours of searching for things. It will dramatically cut down on the clutter of items left out "for now" or "until I find a place for it." Develop a new mantra: everything has its place and a place for everything!

➤ Enlist a new rule: throw out one old thing for every new purchase that enters your home.

➤ When using stairs, never go up or down them empty-handed. Always grab some items that belong to upstairs rooms and quickly put it away while you are there.

➤ Make a mental note to observe what things pile up in your house and where they cluster, and then come up with a place nearby that becomes the official home where those things will reside. Introduce baskets, shelves, and folders for this purpose. They work well. Set aside one basket for you and your partner for incoming mail, bills, and receipts and letters.

➤ Create a number of brightly marked folders for discount coupons, invitations and directions, and other time-sensitive papers that just clutter your counters.

➤ Keep items that are used frequently in places where you can reach them without stooping or bending, and store them close to the place they will be needed.

➤ Use drawer dividers for socks, underwear, lingerie, and tiny items, to keep them separated and organized.

➤ Hang hooks for your keys and purse at the entry to your home, so each time you walk in, you can hang them up.

➢ Establish one defined place in your house for storing library books, and end a house-wide hunt when it is time to read or return them.

➢ Get rid of all junk drawers, or allow yourself just one that you clear out once a week or more. When you establish certain items are being used repeatedly, designate a drawer for those.

➢ ***Things you don't need any longer:***

- Magazines you meant to read but have never taken the time for
- Expired medications
- Clothes you no longer wear
- Sunscreen that's expired or more than one year old
- Extra paper or plastic grocery bags
- Makeup and samples you have never worn
- Cookbooks you rarely use. Cut out your favorite recipes only
- Organize your coupons and throw out all that have expired

- Stuff your crumpled plastic bags from your grocer inside a cardboard roll like a hand towel roll. Keep under your sink.

Getting rid of your clutter and organizing your home top to bottom will free your mind to remember your daily chores. Be vigilant about cleaning about once a month and you will find it much easier to keep up, week-by-week.

The Emotional Toll of CLUTTER

Each area of your home provides you with a unique form of comfort. Comfort and clutter cannot co-exist. Clutter and mess only serves to bring unbalance and will dampen any good spirit. It stands to reason that, give up the clutter and bring in the peace of mind.

De-clutter your kitchen

Your kitchen is regarded as the heart of your home and for a good reason. Here you are nourished and provided for, even if you are dining on a frozen entrée zapped in the microwave rather than a homemade meal lovingly presented by Mom. An untidy and cluttered kitchen makes it hard to nourish yourself and others, on both physical and emotional. How you care for your kitchen is a hot clue to whether you are giving proper attention to your own nourishment and that of others. Cleaning up and de-cluttering your kitchen will open space for you to receive the support and comfort that you need in life.

De-clutter your living and dining room

These are special places where you socialize with family and friends. Here you engage with the world while being at home through watching television, reading the paper or discussing current events with old friends over dinner. Clutter can turn these otherwise special and social spaces into dens of isolation, especially if the mess is so bad that it has been a time since you have invited people over. Look carefully at your living and dining rooms to see what they say about your relationships. Are they important to you? Are you hiding yourself from others, by burying yourself in nasty clutter?

De-clutter your hallways

You need clear hallways to navigate through your home. Your clutter in your hallways prevents important connections between different areas of your home and your life. Look at your hallways and see what it says about the rest of your life. Do they contain good lighting and are they easily navigable, or do they cause confusion and trip you up? If you feel a disconnection between work and family, self and others, what you need to be done and your obligations, it may be time to give your hallways some good organizing.

De-clutter your bathrooms

Each day we use this important space to meet the world. We begin our days from this room. Clutter in the bathroom can mean your don't take pride in how you look and feel. How can you feel clean when using a cluttered, dirty bathroom? A clean, well-decorated bathroom is a tranquil sanctuary for rejuvenation and self-care. Scented soaps, attractive accessories, and fragrant candles all take their place here. This is beauty for the mind and soul. You can beautify your life by organizing and cleaning this important room. Take the time to transform your bathroom into a place of refuge and this will bring a sense of the sacred into your morning and evening personal-care rituals.

De-clutter the bedroom

Your bedroom is for sleeping and intimacy, and it functions as a place of renewal for self and relationships. Clutter in the bedroom is worse than in any room. It is anything but restful and peaceful. If you are feeling "wired and tired," creating order out of chaos in this most personal space will help you relax and to let go of the stresses of the day. Then you will get a good night's sleep or enjoy some special time with your partner. Of all of your rooms, this one is the most critical for being organized and peaceful.

De-clutter your closets

Closets are everything hidden, unknown, or unrecognized. When we fill our closets with clutter, we harness our ability to be intuitive and insightful. Cluttered closets can indicate problems that you may not even be aware of but which block your progress through life, work, and relationships. Keeping the closet door closed is not an obvious solution.

Organizing your closets IS!

De-clutter your attic and basement

A cluttered attic causes you to feel under pressure. It is not easy to feel good about the future when there is so much stuff "hanging about and over your head." Organize those boxes of yesteryear and you will feel ten pounds lighter, instantly! The basement and other below-ground storage areas are thought to be holders of the subconscious mind, so take the time and have that clutter cleaned up!

De-clutter your garage

Think of your car as a symbol of your agility, independence, and ability to be self-propelled in life. If there's so much junk piled high in your garage that you can barely lift the garage door, it is time to organize. Do this and be prepared to move forward in your life, as well.

Stop thinking of de-cluttering as a terrific, and start thinking of it as one of the most effective self-improvement exercises available to you. Every magazine and piece of paper you place in the recycle and every book you give back to the library will liberate you.

Just as giving those older items to charity, will. Free yourself now of clutter and open the flood gates of joy and energy into your life.

Turn Clutter into Harmony

If a primary goal is to exist in a clutter-free environment, think of devising a system in which to operate freely. With a smart system, you will have valuable free time. Having more time to spend your hours doing what you enjoy most is everyone's goal in life.

Using a system, you will have a method of doing something that might otherwise be a strain. You will have a new way of simplifying a task or operation.

Paper clutter is a very good example. We find papers thrown here, there and everywhere. Loose paper can be found in every area of your home. To transform a disorderly area into an orderly one, you will want to first clean up the area of all loose paper and put it away in a designated place or just throw it away. You can use baskets, drawers or shelving space to store away your paper. Once you have a designated place established, it is easier then to remain organized.

Think now about how your paper became so messy in the first place. What did you do with it once it arrived? Did you put the full bundle into a basket, for example? If you glanced at it and then put it down in a haphazard pile at the nearest table or desk near you, chances are that is your problem. Your goal is to designate a said place for every item of value in your entire home. That way you are organized.

The organized way to deal with all paper that crosses your hands and/or desk is to:

1. Have it placed at a designated tray, basket, shelf or drawer.

2. Spend the time you need to look into what the paper commands of you and, when done with it;

3. Place it in either a file, put it in a filing basket to be filed, put it in an out basket, or simply throw it away.

This type of paper flow system will organize you in a heartbeat and will prevent finding assorted pieces of paper everywhere throughout your home. As soon as you receive the paper, you put it in its allotted place. From this, you will create a peaceful work area. You will automatically know where to go to get your paper and where to find paper that you need.

The same system can be applied to reorganizing a disordered environment. You can tackle a room, a closet, or a drawer by first organizing it and then taking a look at how it got that way in the first place. Here is where the new system comes into play. You need to be able to maintain the order you have applied to it for later so that the same mess does not just develop all over again.

The more time and effort you put into being organized, the less time you will need to apply to organizing later

You will need to acquire the necessary "tools" needed to create good order. Having good order is the building block to being better organized.

Shop the discount and specialty stores for great tools to organize. They are inexpensive and work well. If you find your bedroom is hard to keep organized then look around for something to solve your problem. The moment you find the right tool, you can begin to put things into their proper place.

There is no easy way around trying to get your life in order and be better organized. It takes time and effort on your part. The more tools you can apply to your disorganized messes, the easier it will be to maintain order. Once you find the right approach, it will be easy to keep the same momentum going.

Use a system to organize every area of your life. Go from room to room in your home and apply tools to simplify messy problems. You will be so glad you did!

An Orderly Life

There are generally two different types of people who exist in the work place; they are The Organized and The Disorganized. What characteristics set them apart and which do you aspire to be?

There seems to be lack of discipline with The Disorganized. Others around them might think The Disorganized are actually not even aware of the condition they are in, because it is a situation that appears to persist over long periods. Sometimes it can be a never-changing view of that person's surroundings. It is common to conclude that this type of person is often stressed and must go in all directions to get things done, if they can get things done at all.

The Organized, on the other hand, are a unique breed. They seem to be able to create handy places for things. They see to it that "everything has a place and that there's a place for everything." They are the ones you would call on first when you need help to get something important done. They can generally get more done in a relatively short period. They have a real knack for tackling work with a disciplined approach.

Now which would you rather be?

Getting proper instruction and a sense of guidance, the Disorganized can turn around on a dime and become organized. It is often just a matter of providing them with the expertise and then working with them on the discipline it takes to move into the ranks of The Organized.

The annoyances and inconveniences of working around The Disorganized eventually takes its toll on those who know them best. If you work with The Disorganized, you tend to be annoyed by them easily. Often times, a situation creates itself so that others must work harder or bypass the individual to get certain things done. Does this scenario sound all too familiar? This hardship on others can bring about resentment and unnecessary hurt feelings.

The Disorganized are basically enemies to themselves, more than anything, so it is important to change adverse conditions in order to survive in harmony in the work place. Rather than picking up the slack, offer some guidance and direction. This will bring harmony to the relationship.

One of the challenges of The Organized is how to bring harmony between the two conflicting types. To start with, find a way to peacefully get The Disorganized to change their ways. Do this and you will teach The Disorganized to foster new and better habits in all that they do. It can be done if done carefully.

Order to The Organized, is a critical factor for optimum change. Their choice of method is to figure out ways to be more efficient. They want everyone around them to figure out how to accomplish more with the least mount of effort and/or energy. They think always in systematic terms as a way of handling work. They thrive on having everything done in an orderly fashion.

To be or not to be organized - that is the question

The Disorganized should answer that question for him or herself and then act upon it. If they do nothing else, they can ask questions. They can observe and follow the lead. The minute The Disorganized becomes organized, the minute they have more time for themselves. This in itself should be good enough incentive.

Next comes the healing of relationships, where everyone works together in one accord, so in harmony. This is worth striving for. If The Disorganized is serious about changing their ways, they will move on from an attitude of new awareness into a new attitude of action!

Let Good Order Reign!

Even the most organized person can struggle with being orderly. In fact, it is often the most organized who have the most difficulty keeping on top of organization.

What makes the Difference?

As your workload continues to increase, your environment can suffer unless you take some time to take care of administrative and organizational tasks. It does not take long for every day mail to pile up if it is not being put away in its place as you finish with it. That "place" might be a temporary home, but at least the letters are put away instead of sitting out on the desk somewhere.

Remember that whatever is not put in its place will only pile to make clutter.

Because your busy lifestyle warrants continuous maintenance to keep an orderly environment, a key to being clutter-free is to put things away when you are done with them. It really only takes a moment but, if you do not, it can take hours to sort out when it gets out of control.

Remember that time is money.

Your new behavior usually has to be developed, like a routine. Developing a good routine takes time. The act of putting something away right away may sound easy for some, yet, on the other hand, is not part of some individual's basic nature. We are often too busy to be bothered with doing that, right? On the other hand, maybe you just haven't designated a "home" for the item yet, yes? Whatever your attitude is, the best thing you can do for yourself now is change it (the attitude.)

If you were to look around your home right now, it would be a good "drill" to spot what does not have a place.

A new home for magazines could be a magazine basket or holder. For audio and videotapes, a home could be special holders, containers, or even a drawer, or designated shelf. Mail should have a basket to go into. Projects or papers could go in folders. Folders could go in a folder rack, holder, basket, or filing cabinet. It just makes good sense, otherwise, all your items will only lie around and collect dust and this is the first step to amassing clutter. Office supplies can go in a cabinet, a drawer, or containers. Items such as keys and glasses can be placed on hooks or in a designated dish. Now you get the idea!

Once everything has been assigned a place or go to temporarily, the area will be tidy and organized. Suddenly you will think and breathe freely and you will have an increased sense of well being.

It is a good habit to work on just one project at a time and, before moving on to the next activity, put it away.

If you want to be clutter-free, have all of your projects in order. As you finish one, put it away before you begin on the next. This way your work area will remain free, clear, and tidy. You will be able to apply yourself best to your projects in this way. You are developing good habits and you will be more creative. To end you work day, clear off your desk. This will make way for more work to come later. There is nothing more tiring than having to clear the way from the day before when you want to start anew.

There is simplicity in order and organization

First, you decide to change the environment to a better one. Then, you change an attitude. After that, adjust your habits, establish and implement your systems, and lastly, adapt policy to maintain the order put there. It all comes together very nicely.

Getting Rid of "Stuff"

"For the most part, we, who could choose simplicity, choose complication."
                    Anne Morrow Lindbergh, in *Gift from the Sea*

Perhaps you feel that anything that can be hidden away will not be seen, right? This must mean what is hidden away is not in the way.

Where do you we choose to stash away our forgotten items? Usually it is in the patio, basement or garage. Sight unseen, so this must mean we do not need to bother with such items. The bottom line is, all we are really accomplishing is nothing, basically.

The major purpose of being organized is to have a place for everything.

Where do we need to start? We need to go through the decision-making process. We must learn to responsibly let go.

1. If it is an empty jar you need, save a few in your cabinet and recycle the rest.

2. If it is not working and you do not wish to repair it, toss it. You can buy a new one that works.

3. If you have not worn a clothing or jewelry item since last season, give it to charity.

These are some simpler examples that you can use. You can add to them, of course.

You will gain instant respect by cleaning up your space. By waiting, matters will only worsen. Things do not stay the same and, because we are in a constant condition of change, we will eventually be faced with a total mess if we do not deal with it.

The best part of being organized is the amount of new space created.

Anyone can afford even small bursts of time to get better organized. The more time you give yourself the more you will get done.

A few reasons to get organized

1. You are ready to make a move.

2. You need to rent a room or extra storage facility just to accommodate your things.

3. Your closet is full, but you still find there's nothing in it to wear.

4. You want to earn a wad of cash holding a garage sale.

5. You become aware that someone else will end up having to go through your stuff after you are gone.

For some, getting rid of stuff is easy enough. For others, it can be a real emotional undertaking. Memories are usually attached to everything we own and, because of this, can be difficult to let go. However, with a motivated, enthusiastic approach, the task is like wiping down that kitchen fridge so it sparkles back at you. It just makes you feel good.

The Art of Organization

You too can be organized

You like the way your home looks. The furniture that you saved years for sits proudly. Everything is situated just right, yet it's cluttered with paper, items belonging to other parts of the house, too much brick-a-bract, and trash particles that didn't somehow make it to the waste basket.

Take heart! There is a definite art to approaching the task of getting organized. First, let us take a look at why you should do it and what the clutter about you actually does to your decorating scheme.

You have already learned that clutter interferes with your sense of tranquility and energy flow in your home. Objects actually have a frequency of energy, and clutter will interfere with the smooth flow of energy in any surrounding space. This contributes to lethargy and procrastination. You feel weighed down.

Clutter also makes a space seem smaller and diminishes light. This can make you, your family and friends seem depressed.

If you experience stuffy nose, sneezing and coughing in your home, chances are you are breathing in a lot of accumulated dust. This just comes along with the unwanted clutter. Your health will suffer because of the clutter.

Another problem clutter will cause is that it makes a person feel overwhelmed. With so much disorder and unnecessary items about, you will find it is difficult to be focused.

Therefore, along with your energy, your spirit seems to sag. This is not a pretty picture!

These dilemmas are all good indications that it is time to dig in. These are good reasons to put your house in order and get your space organized.

A room that has good order to it is a happy place to live and enjoy. It smiles back at you. You have a place of tranquility and a means from which to focus. When your home is minus the clutter, you have the energy flow you desire. You feel that you have more vim and vinegar.

We should all take pride in our home. Our home should be our refuge away from the storms in life. Our home should be our castle. We should love to be in our home and we should want to entertain often.

As soon as you have a designated space for all of your items, you are better organized. This is the first step and the most important step.

That is the art of getting organized. After you have your entire home organized, you will have a work of art when you are done. With everything put in its assigned place, the area will be an environment that smiles back at you when you enter it. You will feel peace and joy. You will be proud!

Take the organizing plunge today. Do not put it off for one more moment in time. Your time is valuable to you. Use it wisely.

A Few Good Organizing Tips and Tricks

Multi-tasking

Begin today by combining some activities such as: 1) exercise and watching TV, 2) flipping through magazines or catalogs while talking on the telephone, 3) filing your finger nails while waiting for an appointment, 4) watering your favorite plants while clothes are in the dryer.

Organize your kids

Design your kid's room so that they can keep it up themselves. Show your kids how to maintain their own rooms and reward them on their achievement in doing so. Give them their own household responsibilities and chores and then offer them a form of allowance. This will teach them to be organized.

Organize your clothes

Hang clothes in the closet by type, arranging similar items together, and by use. Grouping them by color within the category will make it easier to mix and match your garments.

Store out-of-season clothes in old suitcases, drawers, garment bags or trunks. Keep only current season's coats and jackets in your coat closet. Use closet organizers and you will create more space in your closet.

Organize your kitchen

Here are good ways to add new space to your kitchen: 1) Install smaller wall shelves to hold canisters and small appliances. 2) Store away (or give away) appliances or kitchenware that is no longer being used. 3) Put shelf organizers inside cabinets with high shelf space. 4) Put a pegboard on walls to hang light or smaller items. 5) Use plastic drawer organizers under your kitchen sink to make better use of wasted space.

Organize your bedroom

Add comfort to your bedroom! Make a nifty bedside area by keeping those things you need close at hand in either a night table or handy caddy. This is used to hold items like notepaper, pens, reading glasses and whatever crafts items you like to do in the bedroom. Hang wall shelves on any useable wall space. This will create more storage space for things that decorate the room, or that serve a needed function.

The more you sort through your personal belongings and find a new home for them, the more free space you will be opening up and this is the height of being organized!

Determining your Home-Style

As you begin the chore of organizing your home, it is time to determine the style you wish your home to have. If what you had previously was not working for you, if you had ample amounts of dust and clutter, it is time to begin anew.

Your home should be a place that you enter into with both comfort and joy. When you are properly organized, you feel pride in your home. Your home should smile back at you when you walk in the door, and give you a sense of serenity when you leave.

You can accomplish all of this when you have peace and harmony in your home. Your home environment will be tidy and purposeful and you will draw strength from this.

You will put the harmony in your space by making it look and function the way that best suits you. When you walk into a room, it should look vibrant and comfortable. When you walk into a room that is dark and messy you feel at a loss. This is not how you wish to feel entering into your own home and your friends and family will not want to visit either.

As you enter into a room, you want to feel space to move around. You want it to be free of mess and clutter. Clutter enters your mind and dampens your spirit. It becomes difficult to focus in any area that makes you feel in this way. All you can see is the mess and you cannot think straight. You feel annoyed.

A hassle-free lifestyle will not just happen, you will make it happen. You have to create certain procedures and methods in which to generate the kind of atmosphere and conditions that you want. You need to determine what you want, how you want it, and if you are willing to spend the time and energy to make it happen.

There are a number of important elements at play in streamlining your activities and getting organized. A system can be implemented on anything, just as everything has a sort of "flow chart" to it. Doing household chores has a method to doing them. You must devise that method to be most effective. Setting aside time with family has certain disciplines that work. It is all about how you manage your activity that makes the difference.

If you learn better time management, for instance, the result is more time to do those things that you want to do. The pay off is great!

Budgeting your time is like budgeting your finances. You need to allocate a certain amount of time to certain things. I think we all know what happens when one does not budget their money. We end up without any money (eventually), or we have to scrape up money from somewhere else to make ends meet.

That is what occurs when you do not budget your time. You will end up without any time to do the things you want. You run out of time to accomplish the things you really must do, like organize.

Every element of your life is affected by poor organization skills.

Time is not the only problem we all face. The worse enemy of any lifestyle is mess and clutter. If there is clutter, trouble follows close behind. The excuse that there is no time to organize your clutter gives apparent, reasonable justification for not taking care of it.

However, it is one of the causes of not having time in the first place. There is no "catch 22" situation — one just has to make time to do it.

Visualize about what you want your area to look like. This is a good start. Pour through decorating magazines and cut and paste the designs you like best. This will serve as inspiration to get more organized.

Learn about yourself and what your requirements are. Every item in your home should be there because you dearly want it there, not because there is no place else to put it.

Determine its value and how it helps you by being there. Do you enjoy looking at it? Is it beautiful to you? Does it have a function in your life? How does it make you feel when you spot it?

Too many personal belongings placed everywhere around your home will not provide a sense of harmony. It is the harmony you are after and not the "things." Too many things creates an overwhelming environment that can be stressful, not to mention time consuming in having to clean then time after time. By lessening the amount of personal things in your space, you will achieve the harmony you need. You will have a pleasing combination of elements in a whole.

Creating an organized life at home works in the same fashion at your place of employment.

You need to be in an area that helps you to concentrate and focus. You need to operate with systems that help you to improve your efficiency and productivity. When these elements are in place, it keeps stress levels lower for everyone in your family.

By determining the kind of environment you want to live in, you will achieve the first step to having it that way.

Organizing for a harmonic lifestyle at home requires that you put things in order that are meaningful to you and your family. Remember to always keep it simple. Your home can be a place that you truly enjoy. It can be a showcase of where you live your life with purpose and meaning. Others will take note and will want to come over and share your home with you. It will be a pleasant place to visit, share, and make new friends.

Your well-organized home provides a harmonic environment. The harmony and peace will affect everything that you do. You will rest and play with new meaning and purpose. You will feel better about yourself.

Put the harmony back into your personal space by first defining your home-style. Next, have every room looking functional and orderly with no clutter. Do this and you will feel like a million dollars!

Clever Home and Family Management

For Better Organization

Have you ever stopped to imagine what your home and family life would be like if you ran it like a business?

If you look at the standard operating systems that are employed at work, you will see that there are certain procedures in carrying out various activities.

Take up methodical and organized procedures that help you run your family like an organization. Your household will run smoothly if you also involve other family members in sharing responsibilities. Engage everyone, in one facet or another. This is known as delegating.

What is involved in running your family and home like a business?

Each job assigned must be clearly defined. Depending on your child's age and skills, they will be proud to contribute, and they will learn responsibility in the process. Children will even begin to take care of their rooms better when they are in charge of it. This may not happen overnight, but it will happen in time.

To establish a good working foundation, set up a home base of operation.

This will be the place where you administrate papers, schedules, telephone numbers, and other daily details. This can be located anywhere, so long as all administrative items are centralized. You will not find a successful business with some papers on a desk, other papers in a bathroom, and a few scattered throughout the lunchroom.

There are a number of organizational solutions to put into effect in the household. If there is a particular problem area, a system can be adapted to solve the problem. In other words, if something does not work well, fix it. Come up with a method or system that will keep the problem from reoccurring.

For example, if you keep running out of certain bathroom items, put a pen and pad on the towel rack for you and others to mark down items that need to be purchased at the grocery store. If messages are not relayed, keep a message pad by each telephone to insure messages are recorded and placed in a certain rank. If you can't keep track of family member's activities and events, post a calendar and have each person (who is old enough) responsible for adding their new events.

Create organized procedures and methods in your home and you will become organized. Take a look at your needs as a family unit now.

Have Time on your Side

Perhaps you are like me and you are tired of hearing everyone give you advice about time. They just go on and on. Like, hope you can find some time. On the other hand, do not forget to make yourself some time. How about, do not lose any time. Alternatively, do not waste time. In addition, my all time favorite is, be sure to use time wisely. If I hear just one more I am sure, I will lose it!

Now, they may all be sound advice but what I really want to hear just once is, how about some playtime. That kind of time I do deserve.

You and I can actually accomplish a lot more if we just learn to devote time for ourselves. Doing this, though, is not always so easy.

We should all work very hard and when we do, we are bound to struggle through the pressures of life. It just makes sense. You are likely among those who are often found trying to get ahead and meet the demands of your job or family, right? Yet, if we do not stop and give ourselves the attention we need, we will all end up suffering to one degree or another.

Keep in mind that there is no one right way to manage this. Everyone has variable circumstances. We all have some unique problems in doing or achieving this aim. Perhaps the first thing to realize is that you are not managing time to do this. You are managing yourself.

A well-managed individual is well organized.

In order to manage yourself, establish your priorities. I am not talking about those "most important" things to do. It is prioritizing those things that are most important to you at a personal level. In focusing less on the tangible and more on the fulfillment of things you value, you will then achieve a sense of balance. You just need to determine what those activities are.

Take a look at what your leisure desires are. Travel? Reading? Bowling? Dancing? Dining out more? Visiting with family and friends? Deciding what you want to do is the first step to finding the time to do it.

Your priorities can therefore encompass: Friends and family relations, personal enrichment, health and wellness, pursuing personal passions, and working toward long-range goals. Life is more fulfilling when you are doing those things because they bring you joy. You do not need to sacrifice career, family, and well being to achieve balance in your life. You do not even need to change jobs either. Just change yourself. That should be priority number one.

You can create your own brand in lifestyle. It is not something created for you, I know you might think that others control your life, and that you are not in control, but that just is not true. You have many different choices.

Part of the choices that you will make has to do with doing those things that align with your purpose or spirit. You can opt to take any task and turn it into a purposeful one, giving it importance and meaning. If you do it any other way, it is just a chore. The way you view your activities has a great deal of impact on how you approach them.

Time to gain a whole new perspective

Start by looking at how your activities align with your vision and goals. For example, you can view that boring job as the job that provides for your family. Alternatively, you might view the chore of exercise as a way of staying healthy for those who love and rely on you.

Keep the following things in mind when recreating the structure of your life:

- Focus on enjoying more activities that are in accord with your purpose.
- Schedule each of your priorities and say no to things that do not align with your purpose.
- When planning your schedule, take note of those activities that get you from where you are now to where you want to be.

The goal is in not making work the center of your universe. Step off the "work speedway" even temporarily and regain a sense of balance. Separate what is important to you in your personal life. Those are your priorities at this stage.

Try this for one month: Develop a personal agenda that includes "your time" for family, friends, health, and your passions. Allot various times of the day and week for certain activities, and stick to it as best you can manage. If you find that a work activity has to cut into your time, make an adjustment, but do not make this part of your new habit or routine.

Organize a Bit at a Time

Organize your junk drawer

It is easy to transform junk drawers into neatly organized compartments.

* The first big step to organizing a drawer is creating dividers. This will be easy.

You will need cardboard, scissors and shelf paper. Start by cutting strips of cardboard to size and cover them with shelf paper. Leave a wee notch on each of the ends so that the cardboard dividers can interlock.

* Use an egg carton for the little items that end up in a junk drawer. This will keep your items tidy. It also helps keep visual order in the drawer so that you can instantly see what is in each small space.

* Purchase a pre-assembled utility basket or even a utensil holder that matches the dimensions of your drawer to quickly begin to get things in good order.

• Place all similar items together in clear plastic bags to allow you to see them easily. Film canisters can be used to collect small items such as change, tacks and buttons.

Organize your laundry room

It is a breeze to clean up that messy laundry area, remove some of the clutter, and save loads of time.

* Clear out all of the clutter and remove everything but the machines and large furniture.

* Locate a good sorting area. If you do not have one, make one! Use light and dark pillowcases attached to the wall or side of a cabinet with a bracket. Use curtain clips to hold the pillowcase in place. The pillowcases are a smart sorting method when taking laundry to a laundry mat, too.

* Use up empty wall space over the machines. Install wire shelving. Install a bar for hanging clothes as they come out of the dryer.

* Store your necessities in attractive canisters and decorative jars.

* Place the ironing board off the floor. Hang it closer to your machines for convenience.

* Where you have extra space, place a wheeled cart between your machines (figure C) for added storage. To make your own, use four 1 x 6' pieces of lumber, cut to the length of your machines, some trip pieces, screws, wheels and a little paint. Screw the front and back panels to the bottom and middle shelves. Next, nail trip to the sides and around the top. Attach wheels and paint.

Voila! You have a new laundry room made to order!

You can even organize your children

As an adult, and as you are trying to become organized, having disruptive kids can be a challenge. These types of behaviors are a form of disorganization in itself, taking time and energy from parents.

For many, organizing your kids to do chores, put things away in proper designated places, be respectful and civil can be a most daunting task. With such frustration, some parents may resort to anger, threats and even name-calling.

Anger might seem to be appropriate at times, but if a parent sinks into a continuing pattern of resentment and negativity toward a child's lack of compliance, it could cause real damage to the child's self-concept and well being. None of us wants that.

Nothing breeds unwillingness and apathy more than being made to feel accused and inadequate. Think of a time when you were made to feel that way. Did it make you want to improve at all? Of course, it did not.

Cooperation breeds organization and organization breeds respect.

Create an enthusiastic atmosphere with your children. How do you do that? Have your children exited about rewards they will get if they clean up their rooms, keep the house tidy and do their chores. Let them know that they are appreciated and how a family is a co-operative unit for the survival of everyone. Bring this across to them in a number of ways. They will feel loved and a valuable member of the family. Teach them to earn their place by being a contributing part of it.

What is the first step?

Bring together a system of effective control using earned rewards and praise which is very precise and reliable for all involved.

Devise a point system that adds up to an allowance that lets kids spend their money the way they want to. They love this! This empowers them! If they want that trip to the roller rink or some other new possession that is really important to them, they know getting it will be a direct result of their efforts. This teaches them value for your efforts.

Be encouraging. Do not make them feel poorly if they mess up, but when they do, absolutely, take the reward points away. Let them know there is always next time, and let them know they can do better, but do not sway in your position. It has to be as real as if they were going to a real job and being paid for their production. The rules agreed to have to be kept, no matter what and they have to know it's firm. It has to directly affect what they consider to be important to them and in how they are directly affected by it.

Those well-to-do families and their kids have so much - too much! It's all there without any effort on their parts, and they don't have to earn a thing. They just take it all for granted. Make incentives that are particularly important to them and let them learn the lesson that participation equals real reward.

Tasks to earn rewards can change, week by week, and with multiple kids the highest point winner can take the pick of the favorite chores and the lowest point winner gets the ones that are left over. Make it a realistic approach for each child according to age and ability to have their fair chance to win.

Consult your child's interests for best effect.

Do they have their own reasons and incentive to keep their bedrooms and the play areas clean? Talk it over with them; ask them for examples of how it could be more meaningful for them. Gently guide them to discover for themselves what reasons the clean room, etc. would serve their best needs.

Personalize. Personalize. Personalize.

If they want to earn extra points to gain something special or to catch up if behind, make available extra jobs above and beyond the call of duty. This will help them do that, such as taking over one of the parent's tasks for a time or doing a special project for the home and family. As best as possible, make everything personal to your child. They will flourish and you will see how very organized they will become.

Rearing our children is a really tough job. Even miracles can occur with the right attitude, good communication and good systems! Bring up your child to respect you and to earn their way and you will have a naturally organized household.

Organize your garage

So many American homeowners live with a landfill attached to their homes. It just takes a lot of work to nudge a car into the garage and luckier still to emerge from the car once it is parked. Homeowners continue to wrestle through the jungle of disorganization on a daily basis.

If you will consider some basic objectives, you can create a vision beyond the clutter that has littered garages during the last 100 years:

When in doubt, simply throw it out

Eliminate clutter-buildup that has overtaken your garage.

Start by having a garage sale, give to charity, take a trip to the real landfill, and take a deep breath.

Get rid of all the excess that not only blocks entry into the home but the clutter that blocks energy too.

If it is on the floor, then it is time to store

The very basic premise in garage organizing is to free up floor space. However, how does one deal with the inevitable lawn mower, wheelbarrow, snow blower, bicycles, and other large items? There is so much to deal with!

One method might be to build an enclosed lean-to shed on the side of the garage. Use dimensions of 4' x 8'. This addition will free up valuable floor space in the garage in a heartbeat!

Another option will be the storage shed in the backyard. Many subdivisions are regulated by covenants and restrictions. One may be required to obtain architectural committee approval before an addition can be built.

This is well worth looking into!

Organize and visualize

Once you can see it, you can find it. Once of the easiest methods is to create a wall storage solution.

There are many solutions such a hooks, racks, custom-made cabinets, and yes, the lowly nail is a solution, but none offer a flexible solution.

Down with Pegboard!

Up with Displawallä! Pay a visit to a retail store that displays merchandise on the wall, and these same grooved panels offer the most flexible storage solution for the garage that is available today.

Displawallä is manufactured in 4' x 8' panels. Made with a durable finish, this product needs no painting or maintenance.

Drill drywall screws into the grooves of the panels into the studwall in the garage and then install. Hooks fit in the grooves nicely, making placement a snap. In addition, the hooks are manufactured in varying lengths from one inch to 12 inches, so a variety of objects can be placed anywhere there is a wall. The look, flexibility and durability are all superior benefits from Displawallä.

Storage requirements change. You will appreciate having the flexibility of lifting a hook from the grooved panel. This item enables one to change or add items stored on the wall for Maximum Vertical Storageä.

Once a folding chair or lawn implement can be seen, it is indeed easy to find. Once the Displawallä is attached to the garage wall, there are no holes to drill or nails to hammer simply arrange or rearrange the hooks, as you desire.

Rubbermaid cabinets

These cabinets are both affordable and durable. There is nothing to paint and nothing to maintain. They are great! All that you need is a rubber mallet to hammer the interlocking pieces together. Next, screw the cabinets to the wall. Load capacity is about 35 pounds according to the manufacturer. Cabinets permit one to categorize items to be stored and used routinely. Place lawn and garden items such as smaller tools, plant food, and pots in a designated cabinet. Then place automotive products such as motor oil, antifreeze, and other lubricants in another designated cabinet.

To best organize your garage, plan to simplify, and simplify the plan. This takes time and effort. Once storage needs have been identified, one can create the required shelving, cabinet, and wall-storage system to best suit your needs.

As your life becomes more complicated, the need for greater organization and simplification will occur.

The concepts outlined above are very basic and you will personalize as it best meets with your particular need. It is a good start to being better organized and you can work through the glitches as they happen. Either way, you are far better ahead of the game if you decide today to become better organized. All it takes is good ingenuity and good planning. You will reap the rewards each day!

Organize your child's study habits

If you feel that you at a loss to help your child with their study habits, there is good news. There are tried and true methods that will help!

1. Create a quiet study area. Start by determining where the best place is to study and do homework, and then set up a study environment. Be careful about where you decide your child will study because whatever the designated location chosen for the study base is, how a study "headquarters" is set up affects one's ability to stay focused. Be sure to include a desk and accessories, various study aids, materials, a filing system in place for class materials, and good lighting.

2. Establish school supply storage solutions. Storage repositories are necessary to organize various school materials. These can include: subject accordion-type files or file folders that stand in a cardboard box or portable plastic file container; cardboard cubbyholes for paper supplies; cardboard or plastic shoe boxes in a drawer to stash supplies; tray baskets or bicycle baskets for paper. Use wall shelves, under the bed storage containers, and hanging space on the inside of cupboard and closet doors to add extra storage space.

3. Remove all distractions. Is the study area in a high-volume area? How often are there interruptions from people moving about? Is the TV on? How about the telephone? Try to be free from disturbances and outside noise as best as possible.

4. Set up a disciplined homework routine. Determine when is the best time for studies. What is the time of day when they are at peak performance (mentally most alert)? Part of learning to managing time is to create a routine time of day for studying, at the same time every day.

Parents with Younger Kids:

5. Create an award chart. Devise a clever method to give kids some incentive to do their schoolwork, by rewarding them for completing assignments and achieving good grades.

6. Use tools to motivate and encourage learning. If you can afford to, get a computer. Research has shown that children who master computers will learn faster. There are many fun learning software programs that will stimulate your child's mind to learn.

7. Make reading fun. Set up "reading time" together to help develop reading habits in your children. Do this often enough and this will become a good habit.

For the older students:

8. Create a school bulletin board. Draw up a vertical calendar chart on a magnetic and erasable board, just like the ready-made charts for professionals that are available in a variety of formats. This board will break down assignments into component parts with specific tasks involved in the school project. This method will teach your kids to plan. Include time to study for exams on the board.

9. Maintain a daily schedule. Establish daily schedule forms to delegate the amount of time needed for the most important study priorities. Allow for blocks of time for study periods (i.e., math assignment, science paper). Include appointments, errands, and time off in each of your days, as well.

10. Prepare for good study conditions. Determine your best settings for study. Do you study best alone or with friends? With music or quietly? You might find it helpful to set up a study group to improve one's studies.

11. Take good notes. Organize for class by taking careful notes and organizing them in notebook binders. Outlining a textbook or article helps distinguish the most important facts and points, helping to build up a good understanding of the subject.

12. Establish visuals from reading. A horizontal or vertical timeline will help visualize the chronology and remember the relationship of essential world events. Build a concept tree to help make notes more memorable and present a visual representation of the relationship among several essential facts.

13. Build an indexing system. Design a note card system. This will cut the time it takes to research and organize your term paper. Establish a list of resources by category (magazine articles, encyclopedias, books, newspapers, etc.)

Organize Your Kitchen

The kitchen is the heart of the home. It is a gathering place, a special place. From your kitchen come sights, scents and sounds that signal the appetite. It is the most memorable place in your home.

Your kitchen might come complete with plenty of cabinets, cupboards and drawers, and some may not. Whatever your unique situation, it's how you utilize the space you have and how you discover ways to add more storage solutions (as needed) that makes a difference.

An efficient kitchen

Use the cupboards and drawers in the kitchen to contain items that are grouped together.

For example, place your dishes in a cupboard that is either near the eating table or near the sink area. Food should be gathered with like-items together, and not spread out into different cabinets that contain unrelated items (or having the same type food item put in two places).

Place your coffee machine on a counter-top above a cabinet area. Place your coffee and tea items together near the machine. Pots and pans can placed near the stove area.

To start with, it might be best to empty out the cabinets, one section at a time, and rearrange the items back into cabinets that best suit "the flow" of how you work in your kitchen. Take your time for this takes some thought.

When you decide you organize you will have a place for everything and everything in its place. To accomplish this you will need organizing "tools" in which to store items. You can browse through catalogs or department stores for ideas on what to buy.

Get away from cluttering the counters with too many appliances. If you use the appliance often enough, keep it out. If not, keep it stored away where it cannot be seen. Consider building a shelf above the counter to hold appliances. This will free up your counter space to work on.

Establish a place in your kitchen to keep 1) a message center and/or paper-related items, like a note pad and pens near the phone, 2) cookbooks and recipe boxes, 3) a mail center...

Organize your refrigerator in the same way as you would any other cabinet: group like-items together. Try to avoid keeping leftover foods in containers that sit in the back of the shelves, as they often go bad and smell up your fridge. It's a good idea to clean out the refrigerator weekly to be rid of foods that have "expired."

Take advantage of these few tips. You will enjoy your kitchen that much more.

Put the Word "Organized" Back into your Life!

There are all kinds of smaller and clever ways to organize your existence. If you are the type that just can never seem to get much done, and when you do something, it never seems to be good enough, then you need to be better organized. Here is how:

Do you sometimes feel that life is just plain crazy?

Try as you will, you just cannot always seem to get much done. Perhaps you are speeding along at the blink of an eye. You need to slow down.

We all move along about ten times faster than we should be. We all must balance things such as work, family, and friends. This can be demanding. If you want to have time to do the things you enjoy, ***organizing yourself is the KEY!***

Timesaving Tips

Here are some timesaving tips to help you get, and stay, organized.

1. ***Use a day planner.*** These books used to be used only by the big CEO's, or the school academic nut. Not so today! Look around for a bit before selecting one you like best.

Make sure it suits your every need. You will find day planners in all materials and sizes. Your planner will help you effectively lay out your day on paper, so you know where you are going and what you are doing. These days, planners come complete with money pouches, checkbook holders and computer disk carriers, so shopping around is definitely a good idea!

2. ***Use a family planner.*** Yes, buy another planner for your entire family. This way, everyone in the family knows what everyone else is up to and when. You can plan much better this way. Consider buying those dry-erase boards available in most office stores. Mom can put her important luncheons on there, dad can put his coaching meetings, and the kids can put

their after-school events on it. Place it up in a convenient location, which might be the refrigerator or somewhere in a high-traffic area.

3. **Learn to just say "no."** You are only one person, after all and you cannot do it all! Exercise your stress management techniques by saying "no" occasionally when you are asked to do things that are of little priority to you.

4. **Take time to enjoy yourself.** What makes you the happiest? Spending time with your children? Going out to the movies? Indulging at the spa? Attending sports or shows?

Take a minute to think of what you love to do most and then get out there and do it all! Schedule some **"me time"** in that great new planner you have bought and treat it like an appointment with self! Although doing something such as gardening may sound like a bit of a chore, if you find it relaxing, pencil it in. Everything has a time of its own so make time for yourself.

5. **Take time to do a good clean up.** When was the last time you organized that junk drawer, or sorted through your fridge? Is it time to catch up? At the same time buy some new hooks and organize your purse and keys. When you walk in the door, they should be placed right there ready for next time. Chances are, you might be spending valuable time getting

frustrated over missing items. Make sure everything is located easily with a place for everything. That way, you will know where to look next time. Perhaps invest in some organizers. They sure are worth while when you find your life just that much more organized. Sure beats searching around for hours to find your keys!

6. ***Establish a good routine.*** Keep writing in your planner daily and keep scheduling time for yourself. Throw in the occasional "no." and get into a good routine. Stick with your new routine and you will find you will be happier and with much less stress.

You too can live an ordered life. Life really does not have to be a mess. Take a few steps to ensure that it is not and you will have time for the things that really matter to you most. You will have all the time you want for family, friends, work and more, and best of all, you will be sane. The number one benefit to being better organized is being sane!

12 Simple Ways to Organize

Admit it! Sometimes you can be overwhelmed by seemingly endless streams of paperwork and wonder if you will ever be able to organize it all. Emails or Ezines that you want to keep, ideas you found on the Internet, school papers, notes of ideas that popped into your head as you waited to have a tooth filled, newspaper clippings... You just file and file and file and then forget where that ONE article was that you needed to complete the project that was due last week! Phew! It is all very tiring.

Being a list person is a great help. If you are busy juggling a 9 to 5 work life, family time, a home-based business and taking care of your household, as well as having a number of hobbies - well it's time to start thinking about becoming a list enthusiast. Time to simplify your life!

WE ALL SEARCH FOR GOOD WAYS TO ORGANIZE OUR LIVES.

For all of the super-busy people in this world, there are a number of very clever and yet simple ways to help organize your life and keep your sanity.

1. ***Use Notables:*** Keep a small notebook and pen handy. Take it wherever you go and then just jot down ideas or appointments or things to do instead of trying to remember them and then forgetting them later on.

2. ***Use Good Telephone Habits***: Establish a time limit for each telephone call and make sure you tell your caller. That way you save yourself lots of stress from trying to end the telephone call. This will also aid your caller in condensing the information they want you to hear. This one sounds meticulous but is a major saver.

3. ***Use Waiting Time:*** The next time you visit your dentist, meet with your boss or while waiting for your dinner to cook, take the time to catch up on reading or planning. When that is done use, the time to sort, tidy or just think.

4. ***Give Thanks:*** The next time someone helps you out with something, be sure to offer praise. This can be to a subordinate, co-worker or to a member of the family for any

effort you have noticed. They will be happy to help you again, next time you need them.

5. ***Do it Now!*** Do not allow for the luxury of procrastination. If you do, this will only stress you out when you think about that hateful "to do" item on your list. You will end up blowing your "to do" list right out of proportion and it will become almost impossible to accomplish. Start by tackling the largest or most disliked job first, dividing it up into manageable tasks. At this stage, the other jobs will be a breeze!

6. ***Administrate Chores:*** Delegate those tasks that you have no time for or team up with someone who can help you most.

7. ***Make a Group Effort:*** Save time and footwork by collecting everything to bring with you to complete errands or to distribute in each room of the house instead of making too many trips. Make a fast list while planning out your route and be sure to plan each stop along the way so you do not have to backtrack and lose time.

8. ***Schedule in Some Fun Time!*** Take the time just for YOU. Allot some time in your agenda and even make an appointment for yourself and keep it, even if it's only a leisurely 30 minute bubble bath or a 20 minute walk in the fresh spring air!

9. ***Make More Space:*** Go through your entire file system and then weed out any old unneeded files to free up space in your filing system.

10. ***Deal with it Only Once:*** Handle each letter and each piece of paper only once. Read it and file it, redirect it to somewhere else, schedule it in your day planner or toss it. Do not add it to a never-ending pile on your desk in hopes that you will get to it eventually. You WILL NOT!

11. ***Be your own Post-Master:*** Use those handy sticky notes to write errands needed to be done. Stick them to your front door or your fridge, to remind you as you are headed out. These work great!

12. ***Be your own Systems Engineer:*** You simply find there is too much time wasted every day on searching for things. Find a new *system* that works for you and your lifestyle and then apply it to absolutely everything! Use it like clockwork and you will find new time slots you never thought existed!

C.O.P.E.

C.O.P.E. with Organizing your Life

Whenever it comes to balancing a family, including young children, a home and perhaps a career to boot, you have choices. If you find that your workload sometimes seems like it is just too much, take heart!

From an outside perspective, I would say that the secret to success in organizing is the ability to prioritize your various commitments, enlist the help of others, and not sweat the small stuff.

PRACTICE THE C.O.P.E METHOD

Do you feel overwhelmed? If you want good time management skills, practice the COPE method.

COPE* is an acronym for *Capitalize, Organize, Prioritize, and Energize.

➢ ***Capitalize*** on the ability of every child to help with household chores such as setting the table, clearing the dishes and vacuuming the floor. Train them very early to put away their toys and make their own beds. Put all of your perfectionist tendencies aside while the kids are growing up. Do more with your children and less for your children. If you do all of this, you will be blessed.

➢ ***Organize*** your home to make it easier to locate and store things. Large shelves or a huge toy chest and hangers placed where children can reach them are good examples. Keep things in see-through containers, hang an essential rack on the wall, keep storage bins on casters beneath the beds and then centrally locate a lost and found basket to stash items left lying around the house.

➢ ***Prioritize*** each of your tasks. You cannot do everything but you can do lots. Pick the most important activity and then concentrate on getting it done. If something falls through the cracks, let it be the laundry but not the family outing. Do what is really important, not simply the things that need to be done.

➢ ***Energize*** yourself by getting plenty of rest, eat all of the right foods and adhere to an exercise program. Being physically fit and mentally alert will allow you to handle those stressful situations, which always pop up. Do not do chores at the expense of sleep time. Let the house collapse all around you before you do.

ORGANIZE YOUR MOVE

Organizing your move is much easier than you would think!

Moving is a wonderful opportunity to get organized! It is time to un-jam closets or cupboards, un-dump drawers and anything else that is hidden away. Even the most organized person will occasionally have to return to unused or unseen items to remember they own them in the first place.

Moving is the time to go through all of your "stuff". Some you will keep, some you will give away and lots you will trash! Take the extra time as you are packing to review what you own and make sure everything is something you will find necessary and useful in you new life. If it does not cut the mustard, it is time to throw it away.

You may even find you can "lighten the load" saving you packing time and moving costs as you find things you no longer need.

Keep the stuff someone else will find usable so give to charity as you leave. This can all be a very uplifting experience, honest it can!

Now, start packing by area. This will make unpacking much easier once you arrive. Keep your linen closet items together, bathroom items together, tools or garage items in as many boxes as is necessary.

It is that simple!

Moving can be traumatic or it can be a new adventure for the whole family.

Organize your Home Office

Establish an Organized Home Office

Follow the lead of a well-organized home office. Using the checklist below, incorporate many of the organizing tips found on the list. You will have both a professional and efficient home office.

ORGANIZE YOUR BOOKKEEPING

- Prepare and send invoices to clients
- Enter monthly transactions into bookkeeping software
- Reconcile bank, credit card, and other account statements
- Send reminders for paying bills on their due dates
- Write and prepare checks to be signed to pay bills

ORGANIZE YOUR DATABASE MANAGEMENT

- Enter business card data into a database
- Send an introductory letter to new prospect leads
- Send scheduled marketing pieces to clients and prospects
- Track marketing efforts and summarize the results in a report
- Send regular follow-ups, reminders, and communications to clients
- Call people for missing contact information
- Send fax and email broadcasts

ORGANIZE YOUR DESKTOP PUBLISHING

- Design and print brochures and business cards
- Create flyers, price lists, and other marketing documents
- Lay out, printing, and mailing regular client newsletters
- Prepare professional-looking certificates for seminar participants
- Print labels using company logos or clip art

ORGANIZE YOUR INTERNET SERVICES

* Maintain a newsletter subscription database
* Post announcements and newsletter issues to the list
* Perform an internet search for an item or piece of information
* Edit or upload new information to a website

ORGANIZE YOUR MAIL AND EMAIL SERVICES

- Retrieve email and mail, sort, and *get rid of junk*
- Respond to routine email requests
- Forward items of importance to the client for attention
- Track and forward urgent issues while client is out of town
- Prepare packages and mail out products as orders arrive

ORGANIZE YOUR MARKETING SERVICES

- Send out the appropriate sales brochures for inquiries
- Create and mail a customer feedback questionnaire
- Track the responses to this questionnaire
- Summarize the responses and suggestions in a report

ORGANIZE YOUR PERSONNEL SERVICES

- Send reminders for annual performance reviews
- Prepare or update resumes and introduction letters
- Review resumes and summarize each in a short biography
- Sort resumes for a job according to pre-arranged criteria

ORGANIZE YOUR PRESENTATIONS

- Prepare PowerPoint slides from sketches of diagrams and charts
- Send questionnaires to seminar participants before the talk
- Track completed questionnaires and call non-responders
- Summarize the questionnaire results in a report

ORGANIZE YOUR RESEARCH

- Research potential locations for an upcoming seminar
- Find which locations have the appropriate dates available

- Find which can accommodate the size and type of event
- Research the services available (decorating, food, entertainment)
- Obtain written quotes and specifications from each location
- Monitor periodicals and clip articles of interest
- Visit the library to copy specific articles

ORGANIZE YOUR SECRETARIAL SERVICES

- Confirm upcoming appointments
- Schedule or reschedule appointments
- Get directions for a meeting or appointment
- Store back-up computer tapes for safekeeping
- Track birthdays, anniversaries, and other important dates
- Send out the appropriate cards or gifts for special events
- Manage lists of necessary office supplies and ordering refills
- Coordinate air travel, car rental, and hotel reservations

ORGANIZE YOUR TELEPHONE AND FAX SERVICES

- Receive telephone calls while a client is out of town
- Forward important messages that require immediate attention
- Retrieve voice messages and responding to routine requests
- Receive and handle faxes while a client is out of town

ORGANIZE YOUR TRANSCRIPTION SERVICES

- Type letters and memos from tape or handwritten notes
- Type legal transcripts from cassette tape
- Type medical reports from tape or handwritten notes

ORGANIZE YOUR WORD PROCESSING

- Type handwritten notes from a meeting or seminar
- Type letters, printing on stationery, addressing, and mailing
- Proofread, edit, and check spelling / grammar
- Lay out larger documents

Organizing Home Office Tip of the Day:

PAPER ~ Try to keep paper that requires an action on your part stored separately from items that you are keeping just for reference purposes.

Organize your Workspace

Your workspace, like your home, needs to be well organized. Use these handy tips to get your started:

LAY OUT YOUR WORKSPACE

➤ Use "L" and "U" shaped desks for the most efficient workspaces

➤ Store your gadgets and equipment - telephone, computer, etc. - on one "wing"

➤ Leave the other wing free to spread out while you work

➤ Have everything you need within arm's reach

➤ Put your telephone on the side of the desk opposite your writing hand

➤ This way you can hold the telephone and take notes at the same time

- Add a hutch for extra storage for books, supplies, and equipment
- Avoid cluttering your workspace by filing away personal items

PUT ERGONOMICS TO WORK FOR YOU

- Pay special attention to your body - aches and pains aren't normal
- Do not generally bend, squat, or stretch at your workstation
- Place your monitor at eye level - if not, raise your monitor
- Place your wrists flat when typing or using a mouse
- If not, use a keyboard tray or wrist rest when typing
- When sitting, your thighs need to be parallel to the floor
- Your calves need to be perpendicular to the floor with feet on the ground
- If not, adjust your chair or bring in a footrest

ORGANIZE YOUR SUPPLY STORAGE

- Do not hoard supplies at your desk
- Keep only what you need right now at your workstation
- Use a separate supply area for storing bulk amounts
- Store away extras in labeled containers and group like items together
- Ex: writing utensils, clips, notepads, etc.
- Place flat items (paper, sheet protectors, and folders) in stacking trays
- Place drawer dividers in drawers to keep small items in order
- Place envelopes and note cards in a small vertical rack
- Use bracket shelves above your desk for additional storage

Hire an Organizer

IS IT TIME TO HIRE AN ORGANIZER?

You are busy and you feel lost amidst all your mess and clutter.

THERE ARE REASONS TO HIRE AN ORGANIZER

- ➤ Organizing is much more than just cleaning out
- ➤ If you do not honestly understand why you accumulate, it will just come back again
- ➤ Professional Organizers serve as holistic "clutter doctors" to free up the soul
- ➤ Eradicate the cause of disorganization, as well its symptoms and you will be free
- ➤ Create a lasting change in your environment and your organizational habits for a lifetime

6 REQUIREMENTS FOR ORGANIZING SUCCESS

- ➤ Learn practical, useful, concrete information for a lifetime
- ➤ Learn easy-to-understand organizing techniques that you can implement yourself
- ➤ Acquire and learn to use the appropriate organizing supplies and simplify your life
- ➤ Containers, shelving, racks, desk accessories, drawer dividers, etc. all work great
- ➤ Set up proven, effective, easy-to-use organizing systems to de-clutter the mind
- ➤ Use standardized methods for handling paper, workload, and daily activities

3 COMMON ORGANIZING PRINCIPLES

- ➤ 1) Reduce all forms of clutter

(Get rid of anything that wastes time, space, energy, or money)

- ➤ 2) Create systems that make everyday jobs easier

(Develop effective routines and standardized procedures)

- ➤ 3) Simplify daily responsibilities

(Reduce the amount of time and energy spent on routine activities)

WHAT DO PROFESSIONAL ORGANIZERS DO?

➢ They help you change a disorganized environment

(Reorganize storage, home or office layout, clean out the "clutter")

➢ They help change behaviors that cause disorganization (Procrastinating, failing to plan ahead, and accumulating "excess stuff")

➢ They monitor and encourage your ongoing progress

(Offer follow-up visits, phone calls, coaching, and "homework" assignments)

➢ They teach organizing techniques - also keep clients motivated and focused

➢ They wear many hats - educator, resource, coach, and cheerleader, project manager

Take Control of Chronic Disorganization

Jerri felt trapped by the contents of her home and desperate to change a situation that was paralyzing her life. She was so embarrassed that someone might see inside through a window that she kept all of her blinds closed. The dimly lit interior was depressing on the bright sunny days of May. Inside was a waist-high maze of dozens of boxes, bags of empty soda bottles, stacks of unopened mail, and layers of clothing.

Jerri confessed that she had always found it impossible to be organized. She just could not decide where things should go. She had not allowed anyone, even close friends and family members, to enter her home for many years. It had taken tremendous courage for Jerri to invite someone into her space, into her life, but this 29-year old explained tearfully, "It's overwhelming. I just don't want to live like this anymore!"

Feeling totally overwhelmed: that's the mantra most commonly uttered by those who find themselves in the midst of the chaos of clutter that grows with every mail delivery, notice from school, ring of the telephone, arrival home from a shopping trip. The piles grow because decisions must be made, and decisions cannot be made because the options seem to be never ending. Frustration and exhaustion soon sets in, and the result is the despairing sense of being "overwhelmed."

Daily life should not be so hard!

Do you find yourself an unwilling participant every time you need to go somewhere or get something done? Keys just seem to elude you. Your children come to the door, ready to go by with only one shoe. The bills you finally remembered to pay need to be mailed today in order to avoid more late fees, but where can you find the stamps? Now, where are those envelopes to be mailed? You set the keys down to locate the stamps and now, where are the keys?

Chaos and clutter is a circle, a maddening one!

For some of us, this is an occasional scenario, but for others, the constant confusion disables an otherwise productive life.

You secretly think "If only I could get organized…" You have a sense of what you want to do, need to do but you somehow cannot seem to get there. Your place just does not even resemble those Better Homes and Gardens abodes everyone raves about and you doubt it ever will. What can you do?

You have made many efforts in the past, read the books, purchased containers, sorted and stuffed and stowed, but a short time later it seemed worse than ever before. For some reason, you did not or could not keep clutter at arms reach. You fear filing papers away because you may never again find them. Could it get any worse?

Being Organized does not Just Belong to Others!

In fact, "being organized" is not a goal worthy of your investment for its own sake, but "being organized" is often necessary to make other goals manageable. At the very least you could hire a professional organizer and pick their brains for tips and hints that you could acquire all on your own.

Some organizer-coaches have found that coaching by telephone is an additional service they can provide to benefit clients challenged by chronic disorganization. An organizer-coach has experience in both on-site, hands-on organizing and in the education, support and clarification process of coaching conversations. Coaching by telephone has made these services available to those who are in geographic regions with few professional organizers. It is also a good service for those who are just too embarrassed to have anyone come into their home.

Accumulating mess, junk and clutter can reach huge proportions for some. Jerri went with the professional coach. Right now, they are likely on some kind of treasure hunt together. Her professional coach has taught her to look for the gems amidst the garbage and mess and that includes a gem of an idea. Together, they are both coming up with workable ideas to help Jerri better manage her own disorganization.

There are still times when Jerri feels overwhelmed, but they are fewer, and she has a strategy for moving beyond it. She schedules a session with her organizer-coach and knows that the time they spend together will be both fun and freeing.

In addition, best of all, today, sunlight fills her home.

Smart Time Management for Busy Moms

When people complain that they do not have enough time to do something, what they are really saying is that the thing is not a priority, and what they are doing is choosing another activity in its place.

Let's face it, time cannot be managed but people can!

You can tell time to last longer but it just will not do it. So instead of managing it, we must manage ourselves and use our time well. The best way to begin the discussion of time management is to take a look at your busy life and then develop a plan, a vision, or a program.

Whatever you want to call it, it will give your life good direction. If you do not have a plan or at least a distant goal, you will not know which path is the right path to take in your daily life. Whether it is going to the grocery mart without a shopping list, or deciding whether to work full time, a game plan is what is needed most or decisions are haphazard and just will not work so well.

1. *Establish priorities.*

Write each priority down if it helps (and it usually does). This creates a road map to life and will enable you to easily see how to spend each of your days. For example, if you are clear that your priority is to have an outing as a family, then you will be able to say no to activities that take place during that planned time hour.

If free time is a priority, then you may choose to limit the amount of extracurricular activities a child participates in. Set your priorities with integrity and then stick to them. You will also be able to see when you are straying from any designated path. If you are often straying, then perhaps it is time to reevaluate your plan and then see if it is still working for you.

2. *Decide whether you want to be the Chief, Cook and Bottleawasher. Alternatively, perhaps you prefer to be the MANAGER.*

A family manager wears a number of different hats, from chef to accountant to personal shopper to nurse to teacher. That does not leave much time for taking care of yourself. The way to claim more time for yourself is to become a great manager and train others in your household to do more of the work in your place. Then (the hardest part) be brave enough to let them do it even if it is not exactly the way you would want it done.

3. *Eliminate Time Drainers.*

Be realistic about how you spend your time. It sometimes helps to set a timer when doing certain activities to keep track of just how much time you are putting into any activity. A good plan is to work for 45 minutes of any hour, then take a break for some 15 minutes and use that time to watch TV, surf the web, write e-mails, read magazines, etc. Give yourself a time limit for time off and then get back to doing productive tasks. You will feel more refreshed this way.

4. *Dealing with Phone Calls and Other Interruptions.*

Make use of a stopwatch when you make non-essential telephone calls or when you are interrupted by a call. Be stern with yourself on this and you will save lots of time. Give yourself a time limit so you can move on to the next important thing. Gracefully say "I need to take care of something" and then excuse yourself from the conversation.

5. *Shopping Trips*

People who love to shop can lose track of time and can lose a whole day without really noticing. Approach shopping as a chore and not a hobby and you will find time you never thought you had. Shop with a list or even a timer. Go into the store for the things you need only. If you are at a shop to take advantage of a sale, set a timer and when the timer goes off, you are done. Go directly to the checkout counter and then head off for home.

6. *Coordinate Your Errands*

Do your errands when the stores are the least busy. You will be amazed at how many essentials you can take care of at 9:30 am and at 9:30 pm. Banks and post offices all have slower days than others, too.

Avoid shopping on the busiest days and the busiest times and your errands will speed along much faster and you will not be so frustrated.

Group tasks by type and location. This means you need to have your list of errands.

Determine where you can do each. In addition, go to the area where the most tasks can be done. Or go to the do-it-all-giant-super-mega store where you can do grocery shopping, house wares shopping, get glasses, take pictures, and enjoy your dinner. You will save valuable time.

7. *Accumulate Free Time*

We usually think things will pass along faster than they actually do. Leave free time in your day for when life is unpredictable. Also, leave small wedges of time between appointments in case of traffic or other unknowns. If there is no emergency, then you can relax, read, make calls, listen to the radio, or sip some coffee or tea.

8. *Refuse the Last Minute Madness*

Always plan ahead for what you will need. Planning ahead does eat up some time, but not nearly as much as not planning at all. Living your life by accident leads to more of the same.

Live with purpose and intention and get more done. You will gain a sense of control when you can quickly lay your hands on what you need and know ahead of time that you have everything you need.

Create a launch pad area where you keep your to do list, returns & receipts, directions, and anything else you will need for your day. Kids need these for backpacks and school items. Make grocery lists so you do not have to stop and think on the spot and avoid impulse buying.

9. *Spell it any way you Like N-O Spells NO!*

Four-year-olds can say it, so why can't we? Stop saying yes to every club, PTA, and acquaintance that asks you to do something. There are still only 24 hours in your day. Make yourself a priority and say NO to someone today! Give back to yourself for a change. A good rule is never say yes immediately unless you really feel you want to do it. You can always call back and say yes later.

When you do not say NO you end up overscheduling and this makes everyone a little nuts. Keep this in mind for children as well. Too many activities may be more entertaining, but it certainly comes with the cost of stress. Even if you are raising the next whiz kid, every child needs time to do homework, go to school, sleep, eat, and have free time to engage in creative play and thinking without be overbooked.

10. Delegate that Authority.

As soon as your children are old enough, teach them how to take care of organizing, cleaning, and other household maintenance. Teach your spouse as well. This will blend harmony into the fabric of your lives.

A Final Home Organizing

Where to Begin?

Bookstore shelves are chock-o-block on organizing the home. They offer ideas for maintaining incoming and outgoing paper, filing systems, recipes, clothing, books, CDs, toys, kitchen gadgets and widgets, jewelry, coin collections and canned goods, among other things. Virtually any home can become more orderly with the implementation of just a few easy concepts.

You can read this handy ebook and any good organizing book from the bookshop and still do nothing. You just think about what you will do. Implementation is the key, and in thoroughly disorganized homes, getting started is the least favorite of any job at hand.

Especially if the home has been disorganized for a long period of time and the same tactics for keeping the disorder out of sight have been employed for some time, it is difficult for the homemaker to know where to begin.

Following are a few basic pointers in taking that first step toward a more orderly life.

"Organization is not an option, it is a fundamental survival skill and distinct competitive advantage" – Pam N. Woods

1. Start anywhere in your home, but with just one problem area.

Choose one single area to work on at one time. Incoming paper is a big problem for some families, for example, and by getting that under control, a lot of clutter will be eliminated straight off. Decide where to start based on the answer to this question: "The thing that bothers me most of all is…".

2. Choose an organizational system that you know you will be able to work with easiest.

Simple is generally best; anything too complicated might become overwhelming after awhile. Remember that if paper management (or whatever area you are trying to improve) was easy for you, you would not be in this bind in the first place.

Visit your library and read up on the system that you have chosen to work well for you.

3. Put together the items needed in order to implement the system.

Organizing paper might require file folders, an in-box, a shelving system, etc. Label folders, establish a family mail center, install in-boxes, and carefully follow all other directions in implementing your new system.

4. Decide on a suitable place for items you have accumulated over the years, which are waiting to be sorted, filed or acted on.

Do not try to do all your organizing first, before implementing your new system. Simply gather your collection of papers, deposit them in the designated place, and work on them as you can - even 10 or 15 minutes per day will work down the pile in no time.

5. Begin using your system immediately.

This will prevent the disorganization from spreading into other rooms.

If you find that the system you are using does not address a particular need, such as what to do with school assignments, for example, make a decision about this straight away.

If you simply cannot decide, then allocate a single place for school papers and make sure they all end up there. You can change your system at any point and reorganize things, so do not wait for the perfect idea before you try something new.

6. Use the system like clockwork.

Make no excuses. That is the only way any system will work well for you.

A disorderly home can become just too much for any homemaker who means well but does not know where to begin. The good news is that you can begin right now, from wherever you are. All you have to do is take that first step and with this handy ebook, you have the tools you will need.

The benefits of being organized

- ❑ You will feel better about yourself
- ❑ You will feel calmer
- ❑ Your world will smell and look sweeter
- ❑ You will be more amicable
- ❑ Friends and family will want to drop in
- ❑ Your spouse and children will wear a brighter smile
- ❑ You will have peaceful dreams
- ❑ You will not stumble around your home
- ❑ People will want to pay you more compliments
- ❑ Your kitchen will smell more fragrant
- ❑ Your soul can breathe better

Have a time and place for everything, and do everything in its time and place, and you will not only accomplish more, but have far more leisure than those who are always hurrying

Tryon Edwards

Printed by Libri Plureos GmbH in Hamburg, Germany